#RECIPESHORTS

DELICIOUS DISHES IN
140 CHARACTERS

PHOTOGRAPHY BY

Faith Mason

Kyle Books

First published in Great Britain in 2017 by
Kyle Books, an imprint of Kyle Cathie Ltd
192-198 Vauxhall Bridge Road
London SW1V 1DX
general.enquiries@kylebooks.com
www.kylebooks.co.uk

10 9 8 7 6 5 4 3 2 1

ISBN 978 0 85783 421 8

TEXT © 2017 Andrea Stewart
DESIGN © 2017 Kyle Books
PHOTOGRAPHY © 2017 Faith Mason

DESIGN DIRECTOR Sandy Kim
PHOTOGRAPHER Faith Mason
ILLUSTRATOR Rachel Ann Lindsay
FOOD STYLIST Kathryn Bruton
PROPS STYLIST Lydia Brun
PROJECT EDITOR Sophie Allen
EDITORIAL ASSISTANT Hannah Coughlin
PRODUCTION Nic Jones, Gemma John and Lisa Pinnell

A Cataloguing in Publication record for this title is available from the British Library.

Colour reproduction by ALTA, London
Printed and bound in China by 1010 International Printing Ltd.

INTRODUCTION

Way back in 2009, over a few drinks with my dear friend Jane, I was intrigued by the concept of creating short recipes written in the style of a Twitter post. The idea posed an interesting challenge: could a recipe be delicious, inspiring and easy to follow using just 140 characters?

The 80 recipes on the following pages are fast, fun and easy, dispelling the notion that cooking can take too long or is too complicated. I hope they motivate you to spend a few quality minutes in the kitchen whipping them up – for a mid-week meal or a celebratory feast.

Use the recipes to inspire your culinary creativity. Trust your palate and don't be afraid to experiment. Most of all, have fun! Reaping the rewards of your efforts as you gather family and friends around the table is just so satisfying.

Andrea x

GLOSSARY

When the ingredients are listed consecutively with a specific measurement to start and commas separating the ingredients, use that specific measurement for each of the ingredients listed, eg., 'Mix 2T smkd paprika,lemzest,olv oil' means '2 tablespoons' of each smoked paprika, lemon zest and olive oil, not a combined total of 2 tablespoons. When garlic is mentioned, unless specified otherwise, it refers to finely chopped garlic. Herbs are always fresh unless otherwise stated. 'Serves 1, 2 or many' means that you can multiply the recipe to serve however many people you want. Below are the short forms used in the recipes.

& = and	EVOO = extra virgin olive oil	pnut = peanut
+ = add	frsh = fresh	pots = potatoes
=parts = equal parts	frzn = frozen	prk = pork
~ = approximately	gingr = ginger	pwdr = powder
½'d = halved	gldn syrp = golden syrup	rst'd = roasted
¼'d = quartered	glzd = glazed	S&P = salt and pepper
2 = to	gr olives = green olives	sesme = sesame
almnd = almond	gr8'd = grated	shred = shredded
aubrgine = aubergine	gr8 = grate	simmr = simmer
avo = avocado	grilld = grilled	slcd = sliced
b.pwdr = baking powder	grlic = garlic	smkd = smoked
bl ppr = black pepper	grlicpwdr = garlic powder	sp.onions = spring onions
bl = black	grnd = ground	srv = serve
blendr = blender	guac = guacamole	sw.pot = sweet potato
br.sugar = brown sugar	H2O = water	T = tablespoon
buttr = butter	in2 = into	t = teaspoon
cauliflwr = cauliflower	lemjuice = lemon juice	tendr = tender
centr = centre	lemzest = lemon zest	tog = together
cinmon - cinnamon	marin8 = marinate	tom = tomato
chix = chicken	mozz = mozzarella	uncovrd = uncovered
choc = chocolate	olv oil = olive oil	v. = very
chop'd = chopped	opn = open	van = vanilla essence
cocnut = coconut	ornge = orange	vin = vinegar
cookd = cooked	ovenprf = ovenproof	w/ = with
cran = cranberry	ovr = over	wh wine = white wine
crushd = crushed	Parm = Parmesan	wht vin = white wine vinegar
cvr = cover	pc = pieces	whiskd = whisked
Dijon = Dijon mustard	pepprs = peppers	whiz = whizz or purée or blend
ea = each	pickld = pickled	Worcest = Worcestershire sauce

BREAKFASTS & BRUNCH

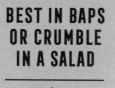

BR.SUGAR BACON

Mix 200g streaky bacon w/100g soft br.sugar,chill ovr night. Transfer 2 foil-lined pan w/rack&cook~180C, til crispy

EGGNHOLE

Buttr sides of sliced brioche, fry 1 side,flip,cut hole in centr&crack egg in2 hole.Flip 2 finish, eat w/crispy round 2 dip in2 egg

PRETTY IN PINK SMOOTHIE

Whiz in blendr 100g frozen
raspberries, 200ml cloudy apple juice,
1t grated ginger, pinch cinnamon

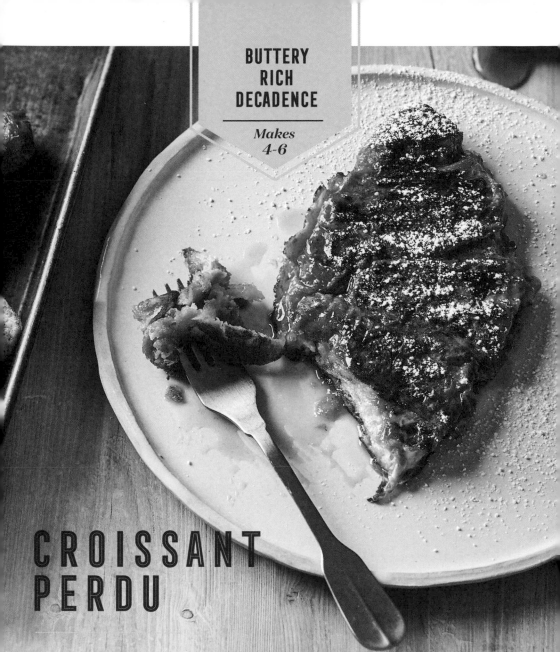

CROISSANT PERDU

Whisk 2eggs,75ml milk, pinch nutmeg. Dunk stale croissants, fry,med hot pan w/knob buttr til crispy. Warm maple syrup 2 srv

SOPHISTICATED
SIMPLICITY

——————

Makes
1

BREAKFAST TARTINE

Spread generous layer
ricotta on sourdough
toast, sprinkle w/
chop'd pistachios
(or fave nuts) & drizzle
w/best honey

SPEEDY SCONES

Mix 225g flour, 60g sugar, 2t b.pwdr.
Gr8 in 60g cold buttr+150ml milk,60g currants,
shape round loaf on tray,200C~20/25min

SPARKLING
MELON

Scoop melon balls&divide in glasses.
Pour generous glug prosecco ovr melon. Whiz
=parts frsh mint w/sugar, sprinkle 2 srv

FRUIT & NUT SMOOTHIE

Whiz fave frozen fruit in blender w/handful
whole almonds, 1T tahini & almond milk til smooth

TROPICAL SALSA

Dice 1 mango,papaya, ½ pineapple.
Mix w/zest&juice1lime, 2 passionfruit, 1T honey,
chop'd mint, 1t gr8'd gingr, eat w/yogurt

MEDITERRANEAN AVO TOAST

Pat dry&fry 2T capers in 2T oil.
Toast 2 slices multigrain bread,top w/slcd avo,
crumbled feta, capers & oregano

CAULIFLWR CHORIZO HASH

Fry high heat chorizo&chop'd onion.
+cauliflwr florets&diced sw.pots,cook til tendr,
+handful spinach,top w/poach egg

MUSTARD GLZD CUMBERLANDS

Roast 6 sausages, turning 2 cook evenly.
Mix 40g ea Dijon,honey &brush
on sausages, cooking through til golden

LEFTOVERS MAKE A FABULOUS DIP!

Serves a crowd

CREAMY RADISH BAGEL

Mix 1t garlic, 200g gr8'd radish, 250g creamcheese,
zest&juice 1 lime,30g chop'd parsley.Chill.
Spread on toasted bagels

SOUPS
& SALADS

RED
PEPPER SOUP

Sweat 170g chop'd onion,1t grlic. +800g tin toms,
5 rst'd red pepprs,1L veg stock,S&P,simmr~25min.
Purée. Top w/ornge zest

**FASTER
THAN
TAKE OUT**

*Serves
2*

MEATBALL
PHO

Brown meatballs w/2 chop'd sp.onions
&1T gr8'd gingr +700ml chix stock&simmr.
+100g cookd rice noodles&generous handful spinach

SWEETCORN SOUP

Serves 4–6

ADD FRIED CHORIZO FOR A SPANISH TWIST

Sauté 200g ea chop'd leek,celery +1T ea grlic,paprika.+500g corn, cvr 1L veg stock,simmr~30min,purée. Top w/fried onions,paprika

SW.POT PNUT SOUP

Sweat 1 chop'd onion,1Tgrlic w/2t garam
masala.+600g sw.pot&300g carrots
&1.2L chix stock. Whiz w/60g pnut buttr. S&P

COURGETTE CARPACCIO

Peel long strips of yellow/green courgettes.
Plate&dress w/=parts lemjuice/EVOO.
Top w/shaved Parm, fresh basil, S&P

TZATZIKI WEDGES

Mix 200g tzatziki w/gr8'd radish,chop'd
oregano&thyme.Cut iceberg in 6 wedges.
Dress w/tzatziki,garnish w/more radish,bl.ppr

CRUNCHY & SWEET

Serves 4-6

CELERY ORANGE SALAD

Dice 250g celery, sauté w/1T coriander seeds, remove heat, + 1T ea gr8'd ginger, ornge zest, whitebalsamic, EVOO. S&P

CARROT CRAN SLAW

Mix 350g julienne carrot w/2t cumin seeds, 3T ea dried cranberries, pumpkin seeds, chop'd parsley/coriander, limejuice, EVOO. S&P

PEACHY
BURRATA

Combine generous
handful rocket,+ torn
pieces of burrata,
grilled peach wedges.
Drizzle w/EVOO.S&P

JEWELLED FREEKEH

Mix 300g cookd freekeh w/2 oranges (zest,segments juice), 3T gr olives, 60g pomegranate seeds, 100g feta. Drizzle EVOO. S&P

TAHINI-MINT PICNIC POTATOES

Whisk 1t dried mint, 2T lemjuice,
60g ea tahini,mayo,yogurt. Toss w/750g cookd
new pots, chop'd parsley,mint,S&P

GINGR
TUNA SALAD

Mix 4T chop'd pickld gingr,rice vin&2T mirin,oil.
+jar quality tuna(drain),1t bl sesme seeds,1sp.onion.
Srv w/avo&pea shoots

'BLT' BOWL

Mix cherry tom halves, gem lettuce,
crispy pancetta, chunky croutons.
Drizzle w/EVOO & balsamic.S&P

SUPERFAST
SUPPERS

MARGHERITA MUFFIN

Split English muffin, toast&spread w/passata,
torn buffalo mozz, ½'d cherry toms. Grill til melted.
Top w/basil. S&P

WALNUT PARSLEY PESTO PASTA

Whiz 2cloves grlic, bunch parsley,
20g walnuts, 50ml EVOO, ½t chilli flakes.
Toss w/500g linguini, gr8'd Parm

ZESTY PASTA

Toss 500g cookd angel hair pasta w/zest
4 lemons, 80g gr8'd Parm, 2t bl ppr.
Drizzle EVOO, sprinkle w/crunchy breadcrumbs

DELICIOUS
HOT OR COLD

Serves
_4-6_

SUMMER
PASTA

Mix 400g cherry toms, 200g feta,1t grlic,175ml EVOO,
1t S&P. Cvr&marin8 2 hrs. Add 500g cookd pasta,
40g gr8'd Parm&30g basil

MOLLUSC MIX

Sauté 1t grlic w/1T gr8'd gingr,3T olv oil.
+500g ea mussels,clams,250ml wh wine,cvr,med-high,
til shells opn.+60ml cream,parsley

MONKFISH MEDALLIONS

Brush monkfish w/olv oil, S&P.
Sprinkle generously w/za'atar, bake ~10min, finish
w/ornge zest. Srv w/herby couscous

FISH FINGER TACOS

Place 1 cookd fish finger in soft taco, garnish w/avo slices, ¼'d cherry toms, top w/natural yogurt & coriander

MR JAY JAY'S SWEET CRUST SALMON

Brush ea salmon fillet (skin-side down)
w/olv oil&2t Dijon. Sprinkle w/2t br.sugar. S&P.
Bake 180C~10mins

JUNIPER
TUNA

Heat 1T olv oil,juniper berries w/rosmary/sage
sprigs.+2 tuna steaks,sear high heat.
Flip,+2T balsamic, juice&segments 1 ornge

MEXI-BURGER

Mix 500g ea prk&beef mince w/35g fajita seasoning. Shape 6 patties, grill. Toast buns, top w/salsa, avo, sour cream & jalapenos

5 MIN PREP!

Serves 4

FAB FRENCH CHIX

Brush 4 chix breasts skin on w/olv oil.
Squeeze lemjuice ovr, sprinkle w/dried
tarragon&paprika. Roast 180C uncovrd~30min

A VERSTAILE RUB!
TRY ON PRAWNS
OR PORK

Serves
4

MASALA ORNGE DUCK

Mix 1T ea garam masala,sesame seeds,½t ea
grlic pwdr,grnd gingr,2T ea ornge juice/zest,EVOO.
Brush ovr 4 cookd duck breasts

EASY APRICOT CHIX

Pour 250g apricot jam ovr 1kg chix thighs/drumstix,
bake 180C uncovrd~45mins/1hr til fully cooked.
Serve w/creamy polenta

FIGGY PIGGY

Brown 4 prk loin chops. Set aside. Fry 1 slcd onion.
Stir in 4T ea fig&plum jams&grainy mustard,H2O.
Add chops, fry ~5/10mins.S&P

EASY
ENTERTAINING

PRAWN GUAC

Mash 2 avo, ¼t ea grlic,chilli flakes,salt
+2T ea lime juice,frsh coriander. Mix in 100g chop'd
cookd prawns. Srv w/tortilla chips

FETA DIP

Whiz 200g feta w/100g ea ricotta & rst'd red pepprs, 30ml lemjuice, glug EVOO+1t ea fresh thyme,oregano &chilli flakes

AVO&WHITE BEAN DIP

Whiz 1tin cannellini beans,1 avo, ½t garlic, handful fresh parsley, 4T ea lemjuice,EVOO. Season w/sea salt

WARM ARTICHOKE DIP

Drain&pulse 1tin artichoke hearts w/200g ea mayo,gr8'd Parm, ¼t grlic pwdr,2T parsley. Ovenprf dish, bake 180C~45min

KALE
CHIPS

Coat kale leaves w/olv oil. S&P. Lay on baking
sheet, no overlap. Bake&shake to ensure
even cooking 200C~9min

GOOEY
GOODNESS

Serves
4

FONTINA FONDU

Gr8 175g Fontina cheese in 22cm castiron pan.
Top w/sliced grlic,chilli flakes,rosemary,S&P,
grill til bubbly. Srv w/bread

FENNEL
TAPENADE

Chop200g fennel,toss w/oil,
S&P,roast200C~20mins.
Pulse w/45g pinenuts,60g gr olives,
1T ea capers,parsley,grlic,
lemzest&EVOO

SOUSED ONIONS

Pour boiling H2O ovr very thinly slcd red onions & place in container. Cover w/white wine vin, ½t ea salt,sugar. Rest 1 hour

STILTON PATÉ

Pulse in food processor 100g ea stilton,cream cheese &buttr w/1t bl ppr, chill. Srv w/water biscuits & v. thinly sliced pear

Serves 6-8

SIMPLE STUNNING CANAPE

BETTER THAN GARLIC BREAD

Makes 1 baguette

SAGE
HOT
BREAD

Slice baguette. Blend 60g saltd buttr w/zest of 1 lemon& 1t dried sage. Buttr ea slice,reshape loaf,wrap w/foil&warm 2 srv

SOCCA

Whisk 100g gram
flour,125ml H2O,
2T olv oil,1t salt.
Rest 60min. Heat
2T oil 2 smoke,lrg
pan, pour battr, bake
300C~15min til goldn

**Makes
1**

**ADD ROSEMARY
FOR HERBY
FLAVOUR**

BLACK
OLIVE
DIP

Whiz 70g bl olives,
1anchovy,1t ea capers,grlic,
1Tparsley+60ml EVOO.
Add 10ml ea redwine vin,
lemjuice & season w/bl ppr

ASPARAGUS BUNDLES

Wrap tog middle section
3 asparagus w/Parma
ham,repeat. Roast 200C
~15mins til tendr, sprinkle
w/gr8'd Parm, bake 2mins

GRILLED
CHICORY

Split chicory in ½ lengthwise, lightly oil,S&P.
Grill til charred&tendr. Top w/Gorgonzola, grill.
Drizzle w/balsamic&EVOO

CAVOLO NERO &BURRATA

Sauté cavolo nero w/slcd grlic til tendr.
Portion in pan,top w/torn burrata,cvr 2 warm,
drizzle w/EVOO. S&P

FIRE UP THE Q!

Serves 2

SOY GLAZE PORK

Marin8 2 pork chops, 4hrs in 6T soy,
2T ea H2O&br.sugar, dash Worcest, 2crushd grlic.
BBQ, baste w/sauce, srv w/sw.pot fries

HOT, SWEET, SOUR & SALTY!

Makes 12 prawns

FIRE PRAWNS

Melt 2T buttr,sriracha, slcd grlic, med-high heat.
+12 shell-on king prawns,cook~5min til pink.
Srv w/chop'd parsley,lemon wedges

TANDOORI LAMB CUTLETS

Mix 100g tandoori paste w/100g natural yogurt.
Add 500g lamb cutlets,marin8 24hrs. Best on BBQ
or grill hot oven

TZATZIKI

Mix 160g gr8'd cucumber, 100g natural yogurt,
1 clove chop'd grlic, 1t dried mint,
1t lemjuice. S&P

Serves
4

**MEDITERRANEAN
MOTHER SAUCE**

SMOKY BEEF SKEWERS

Mix 2T ea smkd paprika,lemzest,olv oil
w/1T ea grlic,dried mint.S&P. Rub in2
500g diced beef,marin8 ovrnight.Skewer&grill

SIMPLE
SIDES

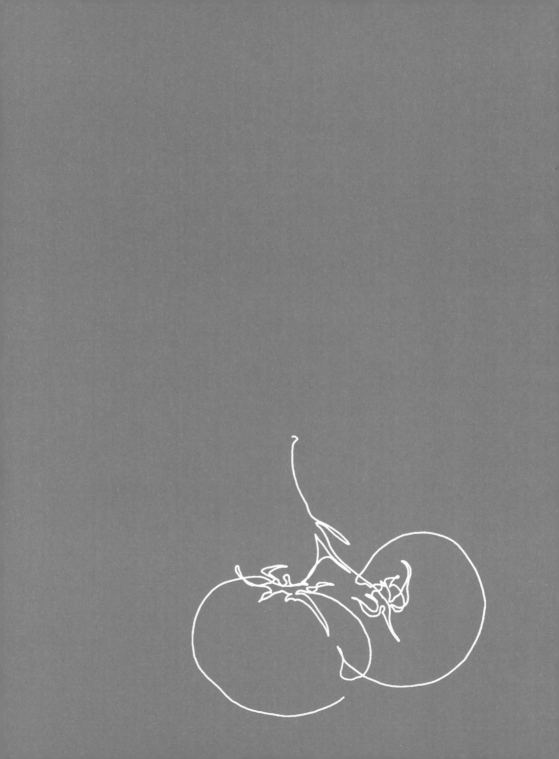

ALSO USE AS A
SMOKEY STEAK
BUTTER

Makes
6

SWEETCORN & SMKD PAPRIKA BUTTER

Mix 1t smkd paprika w/60g soft salted buttr.
Grill or boil 6 corn cobs. Spread w/buttr
& garnish w/coriander

SMASHED CELERIAC

Peel&chop celeriac,cvr
w/vegstock,simmr til soft
~15mins, drain,mash w/
1T buttr, 150g cookd bulgur,
15g chop'd parsley. S&P

VEG TIAN

Layer =prts slcd toms,courgette, onion&aubergine in rows, ovenprf dish.Season w/ herbs de provence,S&P&olv oil. Bake~180C til soft

MOM'S BLUECHEESE TOMS

Season thick slcd toms w/S&P,sugar&dried basil.
Mix 20g ea breadcrumbs,bluecheese per tom,
top toms,bake180C til golden

TRY SALT
BAKING
WHOLE FISH

Serves 4-6

SALTBAKE BEETROOT

Mix 1kg coarse salt,3 whiskd egg wht,60ml H2O,
5staranise,zest 1ornge. Ovenprf dish,lay
6beets,cvr w/salt mix,bake~1hr,180C

GREEN BEANS GREMOLATA

Mix 30g chop'd parsley, zest 2 lemons, 15ml EVOO, ¼t grlic. Toss w/ 200g blanched green beans. S&P

TOSS IN A
SPINACH SALAD

Serves 4

BALSAMIC
BUTTONS

Toss 200g button
mushrooms w/40ml
EVOO,60ml balsamic,
S&P. Roast 200C,
shallow pan w/sprigs
rosemary~20mins

AUBRGINE BOATS

Toast 1T caraway, cumin,coriander seeds. Whiz w/350g rst'd red peppr, 2t chilli flakes.Spread on grilld aubrgine, top w/Parm,warm

Makes 300g sauce

MIX LEFTOVER SAUCE WITH YOGURT FOR A DIP

SWEET & JUICY

Serves 4-6

CHERRY TOM BAKE

Whiz 2 pc bread,40g gr8'd Parm,10g parsley,
2T EVOO,1t grlic. Lay 500g cherry toms ovenprf dish,
top w/crumb,bake180C~20min

STICKY CARROTS

300g baby carrots in large pan w/15g sugar,
30g buttr+125ml H20. Simmr cvrd 5mins,
uncover&cook til sticky. Finish w/sea salt

CRISPY POTS

Boil new pots til tendr,drain. Lay on baking tray,crush gently w/back of spoon.Toss w/olv oil,sea salt, roast hot oven til crispy

SWEET
ENDINGS

AFFOGATO

Take 2 scoops of very best vanilla
ice cream & drown w/shot of hot espresso

CHEESECAKE TART

Whisk in order 250g cream cheese,50g sugar,
1t lemjuice,1egg. Fill 20cm pastry case,
bake 160C~30min 2 set, cool. Top w/jam

BOOZY BERRY FOOL

Pour glug of Cointreau ovr seasonal berries. Leave 1hr (or more). Spoon ovr crushd meringue,top w/whipped cream,fresh mint

SESAME CRUSH ICECREAM

Crush 50g sesame snaps & fold in2 500g slightly softened vanilla ice cream. Re-freeze, garnish w/sesame snaps 2 srv

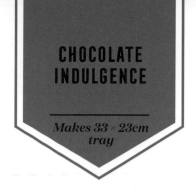

DEB'S CHOC DELIGHT

Cream 200g buttr, 420g sugar,4T cocoa.
+4 eggs, 125g flour. Bake in greased pan,180C~25mins.
Dust w/icing sugar

NO BAKE FUN
FOR KIDS

*Makes approx 14
bonbons*

ALMND BONBONS

Mix 150g almnd buttr w/60g Rice Krispies,
2T maple syrup&pinch salt. Drop by T in
unsweetened shred cocnut,roll balls,chill

COCONUT RICE PUD

Simmr 200g basmati,500ml H2O,cinmon stick~10min
+500ml cocnut milk,4T sugar~15mins.
Srv w/generous chop'd nuts&dried fruit

BR.SUGAR
TARTS

———

Beat 60g buttr,100g br.sugar,gldn syrp.
Stir in 1egg, 1t ea van,lemjuice,wht vin,salt.
Fill mini tart shells,bake180C,15 min

GROWNUP SUNDAE

Heat 100ml maple syrup
w/½T buttr+2T brandy.
Cool. Pour ovr very
best vanilla ice cream&
garnish w/chop'd walnuts

INDEX

ACKNOWLEDGEMENTS

Massive thanks first and foremost to Kyle Cathie, my publisher and Sophie Allen, editor extraordinare! Thank you for sharing my vision and for your patience in what became a very fast moving project. I feel very lucky to have had such expertise and guidance on this book and hope this is the first of many.

Sandy Kim, I don't even have words to put to paper to express how happy I was the second you said 'yes'. Your creative amazingness, dedication and friendship have taken this book from good to great – thank you!

Faith Mason, Kathryn Bruton and Lydia Brun, thank you for your hard work, collaboration and talent. From the get go I said this project needed a special team and you all stepped up to the challenge and delivered.

I am hugely grateful to my friend Jane Francisco – without you this idea (and a few of the recipes) may have just never come about. Thank you for continuing to believe in me and always pushing me to take that next step.

To my recipe testers, Kelly Richardson and Jenny Dulmage, I will be forever indebted to you for your willingness, enthusiasm and honest feedback. Mom, Rony Zibara, Jason Campbell, Deby Taylor, Elaine Clark and Lynn Johnston – thank you for sharing your recipes – they made it!

Gigi Morin and Doug Wallace, you dotted the i's, crossed the t's and I will always be appreciative for your individual areas of expertise and willingness to always help me, no questions asked.

Last but not least, thank you to Michael Clark and Oxford, who never left my side throughout this journey nor complained about repeatedly eating the same recipe over and over. Your endless support goes unmatched. xx